FROM PAPER AIRPLANES
TO OUTER SPACE

by

Seymour Simon

photographs by

Nina Crews

Richard C. Owen Publishers, Inc.
Katonah, New York

Meet the Author titles

Text copyright © 2000 by Seymour Simon
Photographs copyright © 2000 by Nina Crews

Richard C. Owen Publishers, Inc.
PO Box 585
Katonah, New York 10536

Library of Congress Cataloging–in–Publication Data

Simon, Seymour
        From paper airplanes to outer space / by Seymour Simon; photographs by Nina Crews.
              p. cm. — (Meet the author)
        Summary: The children's book author describes his life, his daily activities, and his creative process, showing how all are intertwined.
        ISBN 1-57274-374-3
        1. Simon, Seymour — Juvenile literature. 2. Authors, American—20th century–Biography– Juvenile literature. 3. Children's literature–Authorship — Juvenile literature. [1. Simon, Seymour. 2. Authors, American.] I. Crews, Nina, ill. II. Title . III. Meet the author (Katonah, N.Y.)

PS3569.I4855 F76 2000
509.2—dc21
[B]
                                                                              99-045224

Editorial, Art, and Production Director *Janice Boland*
Production Assistants *Elaine Kemp* and *Donna Parsons*

Color separations by Leo P. Callahan Inc., Binghamton, NY

Printed in the United States of America

9   8   7   6   5   4   3   2   1

To my grandchildren —
*   Joel, Benjamin, Chloe, and Jeremy*
*   — with love from Grandpa*

3

Hi, I'm a city kid. I was born in the Bronx,
a part of New York City.

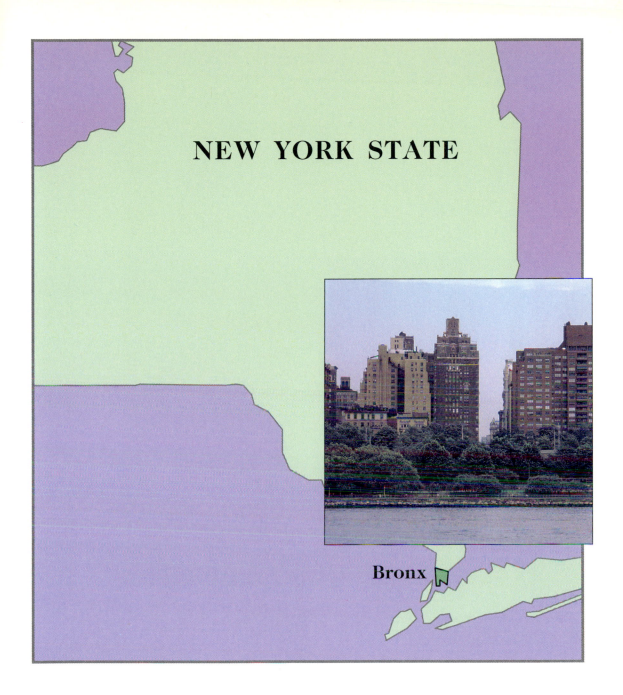

NEW YORK STATE

Bronx

I lived in an apartment house that was five stories high
and seemed far away from anything to do with nature.

But there was a vacant lot on my street.
Trees and weeds grew in the lot.
In the summer wildflowers appeared,
and insects buzzed in the undergrowth.
Birds visited the lot and searched for bugs
and seeds to eat.

Cats roamed the lot, playing in its jungle of grasses
and hunting for mice.

Children came to the lot to play
and look at the plants and animals
that lived there. I was one of those children.
That vacant lot was my own little corner
of country life and nature. So I think
that I grew up a country kid as well as a city kid.

When I was grown up I remembered that lot
and wrote a book about exploring vacant lots.

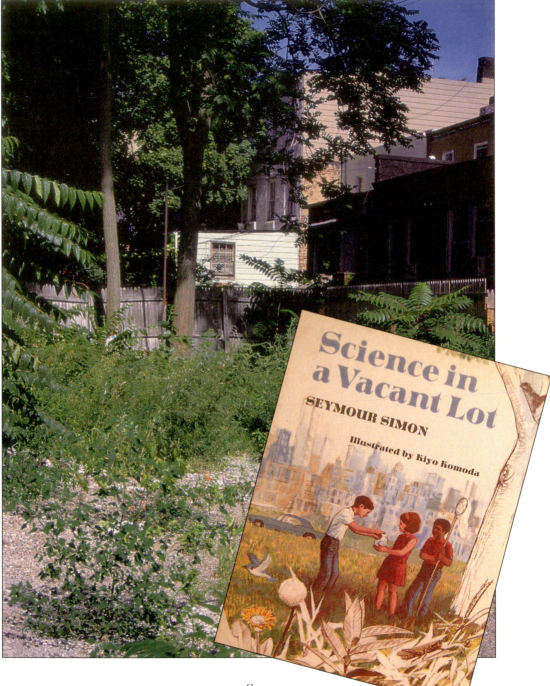

I began writing when I was a child.

I loved reading science fiction stories,

so my first story was about space monsters.

I wrote it in my notebook when I was in second grade.

Years later I wrote a book called *Space Monsters*.

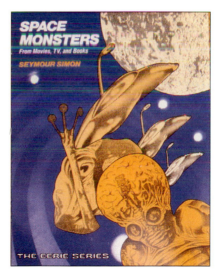

I often write about things that I remember from my childhood.

All my life I've loved to explore the world around me.
At first, I explored what I found near my home.
Then I learned that I could explore by reading.
I read about dinosaurs, sharks, whales, and wolves
and explored mountains, oceans, deserts, and volcanoes.

With books I could explore distant places.
But with my imagination I could go even further.
I looked up at the night sky and learned how to find
the North Star and recognize the Big Dipper.
I wondered whether distant stars had planets
with people living on them.

Now I'm writing books about all these things.

I write my books to help children understand
and enjoy the world and the universe.
But I also write my books for myself,
because I still love to wonder and explore.

There are two places where I write and think up ideas.
One is my study in my house on Long Island, New York,
where I live most of the year.

The other place is at my country house
in the Hudson River Valley in New York State,
where I have a room with a computer and lots of books.

My writing day begins after breakfast.
The hardest part of writing a book is getting started,
so I begin by reading over what I wrote the last time
and rewriting it. Then I rewrite it again.

Sometimes it seems that most of my writing is rewriting.
But I love words and love to play and tinker with them,
so I enjoy rewriting. Once the words start to flow,
I can spend hours on my computer and not even notice
that time has passed.

I usually work from an outline. It often changes as I write.

After a few hours, I stop working on my book
and take a walk to clear my mind and stretch my muscles.
Then I go back home and have lunch.

In the afternoon, I do research for other books that I plan to write.

At my country house there are hawks, foxes, deer, bobcats, and a large lake.

My favorite times are the early morning and late afternoon,
when everything is quiet and still.
Then I can look and think and dream.
I like to watch the color of the water change as the sun sets.
I like to watch the beavers in the lake
and the frogs and turtles along the shore.
I think about how all these living things
are connected to each other and to the world around them
and how I can describe and explain
these wonders in my books.

17

One day a tornado touched down a few miles from my home and left a path of broken and uprooted trees.
That gave me the idea for my book *Tornadoes*.

Because I was a junior high school science teacher,
many of my early books were for children of junior high school age.
My book *The Paper Airplane Book* is about making
and flying different kinds of paper airplanes.
I wrote it because I used to have the children in my class
make paper airplanes and fly them when we studied the science of air.
I still like to play with paper airplanes.

Now I write books about many different subjects
for children of all ages.

For my books about oceans, volcanoes, deserts,
mountains, and the seasons, I go to the place
I'm writing about and take the photographs myself.

For my books about comets, meteors, the earth,
the moon, the sun, and the different planets,
I get the most up-to-date information
from space scientists around the world.
We write letters and talk on the telephone.

I also use the internet to do research.
Then I have to decide what information to use in my book.

I can't go into space to take the pictures myself.
But I get the best color photos of space from NASA,
the Hubble Space Telescope, and observatories around the world.

So that both the words and the photographs
fit together well, I look at the photographs while I write.

One of the subjects that most interested me and my students when I taught science was the human body and how all its systems work together.

That interest has inspired me to write a new series of books. The first books are about the heart, the brain, the bones, and the muscles. The photographs are taken with special scientific instruments that can peer inside the human body.

In graduate school my major interest was animal behavior,
so I enjoy writing photo essay books about animals.
I'm writing about gorillas now and plan to write about spiders,
elephants, and bears.

Because I like pets, I'm going to write books about cats, dogs, and horses.

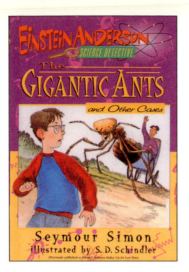

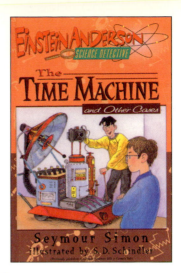

Though I write mostly nonfiction, or true books,
I have also written a series of fiction books called
Einstein Anderson, Science Detective.
Each of these books has ten mystery stories
that can be solved by using science facts.
The reader is challenged to solve each mystery
before Einstein Anderson solves it.

My wife Joyce and I have two grown sons.
I modeled Einstein Anderson on myself
when I was a child,
on our sons when
they were young,
and on some of the
children I taught
in school.

Joyce and I also have four grandchildren who are now old enough
to read my books.

Because I like to read and write poetry,
I collected poems and pictures about space
and put them together to make a book I called *Star Walk*.

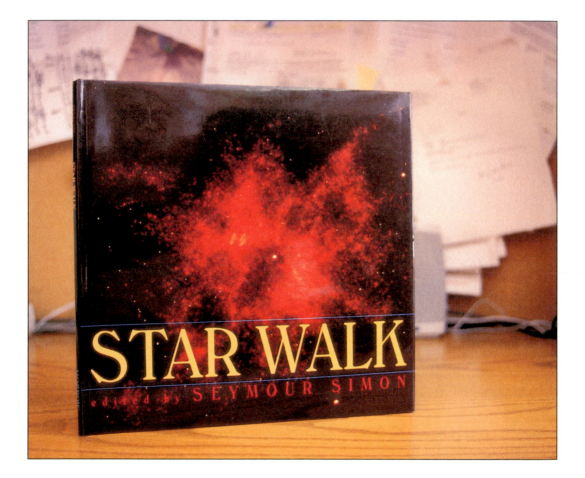

Here's a poem by William Blake that inspires me
and helps me find poetic words when I write about science.

To see a world in a grain of sand
And a heaven in a wildflower:
Hold infinity in the palm of your hand,
And eternity in an hour.

Children often ask me, "Will you ever run out of ideas for books?"

I reply, "I can't imagine that ever happening."

Our world and the universe are so full of wonders
and marvels to observe and explore —
and of course, to write about!

Seymour Simon

Other Books by Seymour Simon

Autumn across America; The Brain; Crocodiles and Alligators; Earthquakes; Einstein Anderson Series; The Heart; Jupiter; Lightning; Mars; Mountains; Muscles; Our Solar System; Sharks; The Stars; Storms; Volcanoes; Whales; Wolves

About the Photographer

Nina Crews graduated from Yale University. As well as being a fine photographer, Nina is the author of many children's books. She spent several days with Seymour Simon, taking pictures of him in both his year-round house and at his country home. Nina also did the photography for David A. Adler's Meet the Author book *My Writing Day*.

Acknowledgments

Photographs on pages 3, 4, 9, and 27 appear courtesy of Seymour Simon. Photograph on page 5 by Richard C. Owen. Photograph on page 7 by Janice Boland. Book cover on page 8 from *Science in a Vacant Lot* by Seymour Simon, illustration by Kiyo Komoda, copyright 1970. Used with permission of Penguin Putnam, Inc. Book cover on page 9 from *Space Monsters* by Seymour Simon copyright 1977. Photograph on page 10 by wildlife photographer Michael Quinton. Photograph on page 11 from *Sharks* by Seymour Simon copyright 1995 by photographer Doug Perrine/Innerspace Visions. Photograph of deer on page 16 by James B. Boland. Book cover on page 18 of *Tornadoes* by Seymour Simon copyright 1999. Used by permission of HarperCollins Publishers. Book cover on page 19 of *The Paper Airplane Book* by Seymour Simon. Illustrated by Byron Barton. Copyright 1973. Used by permission of Penguin Putnam, Inc. Photograph on page 20 of mountain by Seymour Simon from *Mountains* by Seymour Simon copyright 1994 and photograph of leaves by Seymour Simon from *Autumn across America* by Seymour Simon copyright 1993 appear courtesy of Seymour Simon. Illustration on page 21 by Ann Neumman from *Neptune* by Seymour Simon. Illustration copyright 1991 by Ann Neumman. Used with permission of HarperCollins Publishers. Photograph on page 25 and photographs on page 26 of dog and horse by Janice Boland. Cover illustrations on page 27 by S.D. Schindler from *Einstein Anderson, Science Detective: The Gigantic Ants and other Cases* by Seymour Simon copyright 1997 and *Einstein Anderson Science Detective: The Time Machine* by Seymour Simon copyright 1997 used by permission of HarperCollins Publishers. Book cover on page 28 of *Star Walk* by Seymour Simon copyright 1995 used by permission of HarperCollins Publishers. Book cover display on page 30 appears courtesy of their publishers and Seymour Simon.